Math

The expert version

L. C. Norman

CAMBRIDGE UNIVERSITY PRESS

Published by the Press Syndicate of the University of Cambridge
The Pitt Building, Trumpington Street, Cambridge CB2 1RP
40 West 20th Street, New York, NY 10011–4211, USA
10 Stamford Road, Oakleigh, Melbourne 3166, Australia

First published 1994

Printed in Great Britain at the University Press, Cambridge

A catalogue record for this book is available from the British
Library

Library of Congress cataloguing in publication data
Norman, L. C.
Mathland: the expert version / L. C. Norman.
     p.   cm.
1. Mathematical recreations – Juvenile literature. 2. Problem
solving – Juvenile literature. [1. Mathematical recreations.
2. Problem solving.]   I. Title.
QA95.N58 1994
793.7′4 – dc20 94-15713   CIP

ISBN 0 521 46802 7 paperback

Cover illustration and cartoons by Simon Larkin

INSTRUCTIONS

There are detailed instructions on the next two pages.

READ THEM CAREFULLY BEFORE YOU ENTER MATHLAND.

Some of the pages have boxes. These are for you to explore when you have finished travelling through Mathland.

You enter the Dark Cavern of Ignorance.

There is a flash of light, and the Magic Mathematician stands before you.

'You will be given a set of problems to solve,' he explains. 'If you are successful, you will gain points. If you are stuck, you may pay points to receive help. Your answers will guide you to the next step in the maze.

'Mathland is full of the bones of explorers who have lost their way – so choose your route with care . . .'

Use the **map sheet** to record your progress through the maze. (Alternatively, you could use a sheet of A4 paper. Start at the bottom right-hand corner and use a scale of 2 cm to 1 mile.)

Your map should include the names of the places you visit, and the characters you meet there. The roads between places will always be straight – but your path may double back on itself.

You should also record the pages you visit, in the order you visit them. Then, if you lose your way, you will not have to start again at the very beginning.

Finally, there is space on the map sheet for you to record the points you win and lose.

Your eyes make out a dim light to the north. You make your way cautiously towards it, and find a cleft leading out of the cavern.

Start on page **10**. Good luck!

YOU SHOULD NOT BE READING THIS PAGE.

You were told to start on page **10**.

Turn back to the Instructions and read them again, more carefully this time.

You proceed along a narrow tunnel for some 4 miles. At the end you reach the Crystal Cave. The floor of the cave is littered with precious stones. You pick up a diamond crystal.

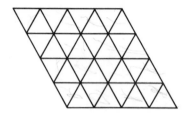

How many diamond shapes can you find in this structure?

Take tan of your answer, round to 2 significant figures and turn to that page ▶▶

If stuck on the problem PAY 10 POINTS ▶▶ 11

If stuck on the calculation PAY 5 POINTS ▶▶ 74

The crystals in the cave reflect your path back on itself, and you return to the Fountain of Fermat.

'What – you're here again!' grins the gnome. 'There are just two paths to choose from this time, so you have two numbers to find.'

Find whole numbers n and m so that:

$$2^n - 2^m = 2016$$

Calculate $\dfrac{mn - (m + n)}{3}$

and turn to that page ▶▶

If stuck PAY 10 POINTS ▶▶ 19

4

You move north for 3 miles. The path rises steeply and you find yourself in the sunlight at the Crossroads of Cantor.

An adder is curled up in the middle of the road.

'I'm sso pleassed that you passsed by,' she hisses. 'You can ssolve a tricky ssituation.

'My father is twice as old as I am and twelve times as old as my pet mouse.

'How many times older than me was my father when I was as old as the mouse is now?'

Take thrice your answer and turn to that page ▶▶

If stuck PAY 10 POINTS ▶▶ 12

(i)   (ii)   (iii)

Make a cube out of card, and mark the
faces like diagram (i). Now see how
diagrams (ii) and (iii) will fit.

What is opposite to the ✕ :

 ?

Count the corners of your answer, multiply by 9 and turn
to that page ▶▶

If stuck on the problem ▶▶ 14

6

You follow the dusty track for 4 miles. You reach the revolving Door of Doppler which blocks your path.

A slimy snail sits beside the door and simpers at you.

'Read the coded message inscribed on the door, and you will know what to do. The key to the code lies in its factors.'

NTEEONXPTTAYTGNUEIRTNNWE

If you have cracked the code ▶▶

If stuck PAY 10 POINTS ▶▶ 18

Many of the places in Mathland are named after famous mathematicians. Find out about them.

'Let me asssisst you,' hisses the adder.

If Anaconda has x mice,
then Boa has $2x + 30$ mice,
and Cobra has $3(2x + 30) + 60$ mice.

So, altogether:

$$x + 2x + 30 + 3(2x + 30) + 60 = 270$$
$$9x + 180 = 270$$
$$9x = 90$$
$$x = 10$$

Anaconda has 10 mice.

'Now carry on with your journey. Follow the road to your left.'

 6

8

You follow a narrow passage between some rocks and reach the Well of Weber. Three yellow frogs and three green frogs sit on some stones in front of the well.

They want to change ends.

A frog can slide onto an empty stone, or jump over a different-coloured frog onto an empty stone. A frog cannot move backwards.

How many moves will it take for them to swap over?

Take your answer and turn to that page ▶▶

If stuck PAY 10 POINTS ▶▶ 25

9

'You should have kept trying,' squeals the snail. 'Slither straight through the Door of Doppler and proceed south for 1 mile.'

 8

This rectangle can be divided into 9 separate, different-sized squares. Find out how it can be done.

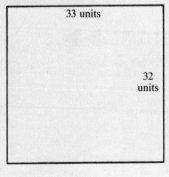

33 units

32 units

After 2 miles you come to the Fountain of Fermat. A gnarled gnome sits on the fountain.

'Three roads meet here,' he glowers. 'You must solve this problem to decide which path to take.'

Here are three views of the same cube.

Which symbol is opposite to the :

, ■ or ?

Take the number of vertices (corners) of your answer, multiply by 9 and turn to that page

If stuck PAY 10 POINTS ▶▶ 5

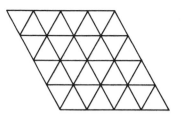

Think about different shapes and sizes of diamonds.

How many are there like this?

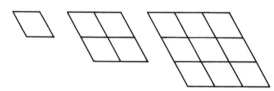

Don't forget the twisted ones:

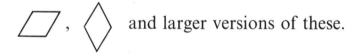 and larger versions of these.

When you have the total number, take tan of your answer, round to 2 significant figures and turn to that page ▶▶

If still stuck on the problem LOSE 10 POINTS ▶▶ 3

If stuck on the calculation PAY 5 POINTS ▶▶ 74

12

Suppose the mouse is now *m* years old.

So my father is 12*m* years old, and I am 6*m* years old.

I was as old as the mouse 5*m* years ago, and my father was then 7*m* years old.

So the answer is 7.

Try a different problem.

Anaconda has some mice.

Boa has twice as many as Anaconda, plus thirty more.

Cobra has three times as many as Boa, plus sixty more.

Altogether, they have 270 mice.

How many does Anaconda have?

Take your answer, double it and turn to that page ▶▶

If stuck ▶▶ 7

'Good,' grins the gnome.

$$2^{11} - 2^5 = 2016$$

SCORE - 30 - POINTS

▶▶ 4

Superstition has 13 as an unlucky number. Find out why.

Investigate the number 13, and the decimal forms of $\frac{1}{13}$, $\frac{2}{13}$, $\cdots$

14

'You give up too easily,' growls the gnome.

LOSE 20 POINTS

'Now take the path to your left.'

▶▶ 2

The pyramid numbers are:

1, 5, 14, . . .

Find the next three numbers in the sequence.

Why are they called pyramid numbers?

'Correct,' croak the frogs.

It takes them 15 moves to swap over.

Now turn through 180° and return to the Door of Doppler.

You walk straight through the Door of Doppler. You carry on without turning for the same distance as that between the Door and the Well.

►► 16

Suppose you have *m* green frogs at one end, and *n* yellow frogs at the other.

Now how many moves will there be?

16

You reach the shores of Lake Pythagoras. A ferryman, Fred, stands at the edge of the water with his wife Freda. Also there are his friends George and Harry, with their wives Georgina and Harriet.

'We all want to cross the lake,' Fred explains, 'but my boat is only big enough for three people, and only I or my wife can row it. The trouble is, none of the husbands is willing to leave his wife with another man unless he is there too.

'How many journeys to and fro will it take to ferry us all across the lake?'

Take your answer and find its square root. Round to 2 significant figures and turn to that page ▶▶

If stuck with the problem PAY 10 POINTS ▶▶ 38

If stuck with the calculation PAY 5 POINTS ▶▶ 74

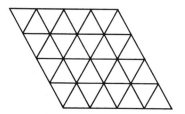

You cracked the crystal!

SCORE **30** *POINTS*

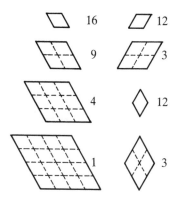

That makes 60 diamonds.

$\tan 60° = 1·7$ to 2 s.f.

 3

18

Think about this coded message:

CEIEANOTSSGODHMSEW

There are 18 letters.

Possible factor pairs of 18 are:

$3 \times 6, 6 \times 3, 2 \times 9, 9 \times 2 (18 \times 1, 1 \times 18)$

In this case, three groups of 6 letters is the key to unlocking the code.

Rewrite the message in groups of 6:

C	E	I	E	A	N
O	T	S	S	G	O
D	H	M	S	E	W

and read downwards:

CODETHISMESSAGENOW

Now try the original inscription:

NTEEONXPTTAYTGNUEIRTNNWE

When you have cracked the code ▶▶

If you are still stuck ▶▶ 9

$$2^n - 2^m = 2016$$

Don't be sophisticated – just experiment!

Start by finding a number n so that 2^n is bigger than 2016.

How much bigger than 2016 is 2^n?

Is that a power of 2? Keep trying.

Calculate $\dfrac{mn - (m + n)}{3}$

and turn to that page ▶▶

If you are still stuck, creep past the gnome.

LOSE 20 POINTS ▶▶ 4

20

'Excellent!' exclaims the adder. 'Anaconda has 10 mice.'

SCORE *POINTS*

'Now follow the road to your left.'

▶▶ 6

The tetrahedral numbers are:

1, 4, 10, 20, . . .

Find the next three terms and the general term.

Why are these numbers called tetrahedral?

'Thank you sso much,' hisses the adder.
'Now I know the age of my father.'

SCORE **30** POINTS

'Now follow the road to your left.'

▶▶ 6

Georg Cantor (1845–1918) founded set theory and
introduced the concept of infinite numbers. His doctoral
thesis was entitled:

'In mathematics the art of asking questions is more
valuable than solving problems.'

'Fantastic!' says the ferryman. 'Now I see how to do it in 5 journeys!

'I'll take them across and then come back for you.'

SCORE ☀30☀ POINTS

▶▶ 41

| 3 | 4 | | | 5 | 12 | | | 8 | 15 | |

'This is Lake *Pythagoras*,' taunts the troll.

$$3^2 + 4^2 = ?$$

Take your three numbers. Add them together, take the cube root, round to 2 significant figures and turn to that page ▶▶

If still stuck on the problem ▶▶ 53

If stuck on the calculation PAY 5 POINTS ▶▶ 74

24

You turn left through 45° and follow the road for 2 miles till you reach the Mine of Mersenne.

Two dwarfs are busy piling up bars of gold, silver and platinum.

'We need your assistance,' they cry. 'We want to share out these bars between some of our brothers. We want to satisfy as many brothers as possible, but each must receive an identical pile.'

There are 42 platinum bars, 70 gold bars and 112 silver bars.

How many piles can be made?

Take tan of your answer. Then take the reciprocal. Round to 2 significant figures and turn to that page ▶▶

If stuck on the problem PAY 10 POINTS ▶▶ 34

If stuck on the calculation PAY 5 POINTS ▶▶ 74

Try a simpler problem first.

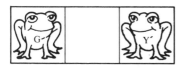 How many moves?

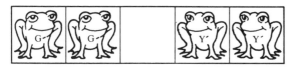

Now how many moves?

Can you solve the problem with three frogs at each end?

How many moves for three frogs?

Take your answer and turn to that page

If you are still stuck ▶▶ 37

YSGOL BRO GWAUN

LOSE 10 POINTS

It takes 9 journeys for them to cross the lake.

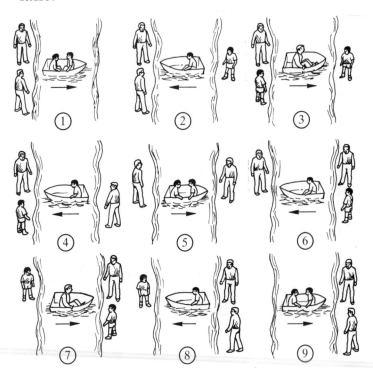

'I'll ferry you across now,' calls the ferryman.

 41

'Good,' growls the gnome.

SCORE **30** *POINTS*

'Now take the path to your left.'

 2

Fermat was a 17th century French mathematician. The proof of Fermat's Last Theorem has eluded mathematicians for centuries. Fermat wrote in the margin of a notebook: 'I have found an admirable proof of this theorem, but the margin is too narrow to contain it.'

The proof was thought to be solved in 1993, using 15 years' research plus powerful computers. It was 200 pages long – some margin!

What is Fermat's Last Theorem?

28

$$30 = 2 \times 3 \times 5$$
$$84 = 2 \times 2 \times 3 \times 7$$
$$90 = 2 \times 3 \times 3 \times 5$$

So these numbers have 2×3 in common.
Therefore we can make 6 piles.

SCORE  POINTS

 31

> **MAP CHECK**
> You should be 7 miles from the
> Crossroads of Cantor. If you are not,
> go back to **24** – did you *turn* through 45°?

Mersenne carried out work on perfect numbers (for example 28) and prime numbers of the form $2^p - 1$, where p is a prime number.

What is a perfect number?

Are all numbers of the form $2^p - 1$ prime when p is prime?

'Super!' squeaks the snail. 'You cracked the code and found your way.'

SCORE - **30** - POINTS

'You may pass through the Door of Doppler.

'Slither south for 1 mile.'

 8

For what values of *n* is $2n^2 + 29$ prime?

30

You make your way south and climb for 2 miles up the steep slopes of Mount de Moivre. At the summit stands a wise old nanny goat.

'Below, you see my Kingdom,' she bleats. 'I have a length of wire 24 miles long. I want to enclose the largest rectangular area possible.

'How long should I make the sides?'

If the shorter side is n miles, take the $(n-1)$th and nth digits of π. Turn to that page ▶▶

If stuck on the problem PAY 10 POINTS ▶▶ **43**

If stuck on the calculation PAY 5 POINTS ▶▶ **74**

You turn west, and continue for 2 miles until you reach the Garden of Gauss.

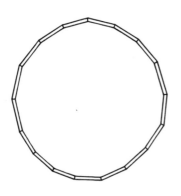

A parrot is sitting in the middle of a walled area. At first you think that the courtyard is circular. Then you realise that it has 17 straight sides.

'Pretty Polly!' squawks the parrot, followed by 'Polly gone polygon!' as she flies round and round.

'What I want to know,' she squawks, 'is, if I draw in all the diagonals of my polygon, how many will there be?' (Do not count the walled edges.)

Take cos of your answer, round to 2 significant figures and turn to that page ▶▶

If stuck on the problem PAY 10 POINTS ▶▶ 42

If stuck on the calculation PAY 5 POINTS ▶▶ 74

LOSE 20 POINTS

There would be $\dfrac{19 \times 16}{2} = 152$ diagonals.

'Polly gone polygon!' screams the parrot, as she flies off towards a nearby mountain. You follow.

 30

Many numbers can be expressed as the sum of consecutive integers. For example:

$$15 = 7 + 8 \qquad 12 = 3 + 4 + 5$$

Which numbers cannot be written in this way – and why not?

'So you recognise Pythagorean triples,'
twitters the troll.

$$3^2 + 4^2 = 5^2$$
$$5^2 + 12^2 = 13^2$$
$$8^2 + 15^2 = 17^2$$

SCORE **30** *POINTS*

'You had better be
on your way.'

▶▶ 24

Investigate squares and cubes, for example:

$$2^2 + 11^2 = 5^3$$

Can you find other numbers such that:

$$a^2 + b^2 = c^3 ?$$

'Let us explain,' dribble the dwarfs.

$$42 = \mathbf{2} \times 3 \times \mathbf{7}$$
$$70 = \mathbf{2} \times 5 \times \mathbf{7}$$
$$112 = 2 \times 2 \times 2 \times \mathbf{2} \times \mathbf{7}$$

These three numbers all have 2×7 in common. So we can split the bars into 14 piles, with:

$$\left.\begin{array}{l} 3 \text{ platinum} \\ 5 \text{ gold} \\ 8 \text{ silver} \end{array}\right\} \text{ in each}$$

'Can you sort our piles of jewels?' demand the dwarfs. 'We have 30 emeralds, 84 sapphires and 90 rubies. As before, each pile must be identical. What is the maximum number of piles we can make?'

Take your answer, square it, take the reciprocal, round to 2 significant figures and turn to that page ▶▶

If stuck on the problem ▶▶ 39

If stuck on the calculation PAY 5 POINTS ▶▶ 74

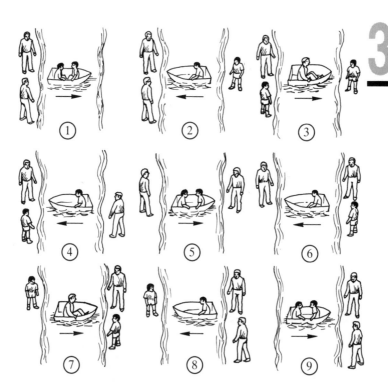

'Fantastic!' says the ferryman. 'Now I see how they can do it in 9 journeys.'

SCORE ✳ 20 ✳ POINTS

'I'll ferry you across now.'

▶▶ 41

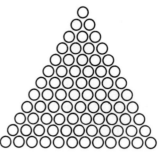

'Let me help you,' drools the dragon.
The total number of coins in the pile is:

$$1 + 2 + 3 + \ldots + 15$$

Split the numbers into pairs:

```
 1  2  3  4  5  6  7  8
15 14 13 12 11 10  9
```

These all add up to 16. Middle number

So the total is $(7 \times 16) + 8 = 120$.

'Now,' continues the
dragon, 'look at that
pile of coins over
there. Work out how
many there are.'

Square your answer, round to 2 significant figures and
turn to that page ▶▶

If stuck on the problem ▶▶ 68

If stuck on the calculation PAY 5 POINTS ▶▶ 74

Practise for another day!

There is a crucial stage where you must slide one of the end frogs, rather than do the more obvious jump. It takes 15 moves to swap them over.

Turn through 180° and return to the Door of Doppler.

You walk straight through the Door of Doppler. You carry on without turning for the same distance as that between the Door and the Well.

 16

'I think this would work,' explains the ferryman.

'It takes 5 journeys.

'Can you solve my other problem? Two men and two boys need to cross the lake. Their boat will carry either one man or two boys.

'What is the smallest number of journeys they need to make to and fro across the lake?'

Take your answer, multiply by 5, subtract 10 and turn to that page ▶▶

If stuck ▶▶ 26

$$30 = 2 \times 3 \times 5$$
$$84 = 2 \times 2 \times 3 \times 7$$
$$90 = 2 \times 3 \times 3 \times 5$$

So these numbers have 2×3 in common.
We can make 6 piles.

MAP CHECK

You should be 7 miles from the
Crossroads of Cantor. If you are not,
go back to **24** – did you *turn* through 45°?

 31

Think of a number.
Write down all of its factors.
What sort of numbers have:
  just two factors;
  just four factors;
  an odd number of factors?

'Good,' declare the dwarfs.

$$42 = 2 \times 3 \times 7$$
$$70 = 2 \times 5 \times 7$$
$$112 = 2 \times 2 \times 2 \times 2 \times 7$$

These three numbers all have 2×7 in common. So we can split the bars into 14 piles with:

$$\left. \begin{array}{l} 3 \text{ platinum} \\ 5 \text{ gold} \\ 8 \text{ silver} \end{array} \right\} \text{in each}$$

SCORE –🌑30🌑– POINTS

MAP CHECK

You should be 7 miles from the Crossroads of Cantor. If you are not, go back to **24** – did you *turn* through 45°?

▶▶ 31

The ferryman takes you, in a north-east direction, for nearly six miles across Lake Pythagoras.

HINT

Think about this triangle and work out how long the other sides will be.

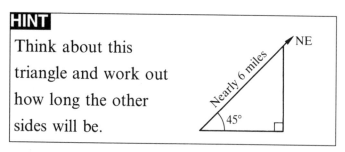

On the shores of Lake Pythagoras you are met by a towering troll.

'I'm glad you've come,' trills the troll. 'Find my missing numbers.'

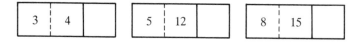

Take your three numbers. Add them together, take the cube root, round to 2 significant figures and turn to that page ▶▶

If stuck on the problem PAY 10 POINTS ▶▶ **23**

If stuck on the calculation PAY 5 POINTS ▶▶ **74**

Each point of the edge can be joined to 14

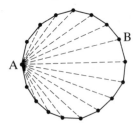

other points across the polygon. (You don't count the point A itself or the adjacent points because the lines to them go along the wall.) There are 17 points, so you have $17 \times 14 = 238$ lines. But you will have counted each line twice (A to B *and* B to A), so in all there are $\frac{238}{2} = 119$ diagonals.

'How many diagonals are there in my 19-sided pagoda?' pouts the parrot.

Find your answer, take sin of it, round to 2 significant figures and turn to that page ▶▶

If stuck on the problem ▶▶ 32

If stuck on the calculation PAY 5 POINTS ▶▶ 74

'Let's do it together,' bleats the goat.

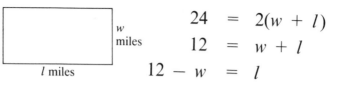

$$24 = 2(w + l)$$
$$12 = w + l$$
$$12 - w = l$$

$$\text{Area} = wl = w(12-w)$$

What value of w will give the biggest value for the area?

One way of finding out would be to draw a graph.

A less reliable way would be to draw some fields with a perimeter of 24 miles, and to find the one with the largest area.

When you have found w, take the $(w - 1)$th and the wth digits of π. Turn to that page ▶▶

If stuck on the problem ▶▶ 52

If stuck on the calculation PAY 5 POINTS ▶▶ 74

44

'You again!' squawks the parrot. 'This time follow the path on your left.'

After 2 miles you reach the Pass of Pascal. You smell sulphur and burning. A large green dragon lies curled up asleep across the path. As you approach, he lifts one scaly eyelid and regards you with an evil yellow eye.

 45

Suppose you have 5 different letters and 5 matching envelopes. In how many different ways can the letters be put in the envelopes so that each letter is in the wrong envelope?

'I was just counting my treasure,' yawns the dragon.

'I've counted these piles of coins:

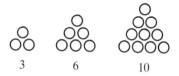

but I need to know how many there are in that big pile. Can you work it out?'

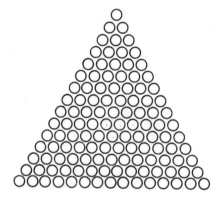

Take cos of your answer, round to 2 significant figures and turn to that page ►►

If stuck on the problem PAY 10 POINTS ►► 36

If stuck on the calculation PAY 5 POINTS ►► 74

LOSE 20 POINTS

'Your brain must be addled,' claims the adder.

The number of spots is:

$$8(0 + 1 + \ldots + 6)$$
$$= 8 \times 21$$
$$= 168$$

▶▶ 57

Dominoes originated in China, and represented all possible throws of two Chinese dice. Some tiles occurred more than once, and the Chinese set had 32 tiles. Dominoes first appeared in Europe, possibly imported from China, in the late 18th century.

'Clever Polly!' screams the parrot.

There are $\dfrac{19 \times 16}{2} = 152$ diagonals.

SCORE POINTS

'Polly gone polygon!' continues the parrot, as she flies off towards a nearby mountain. You follow.

▶▶ 30

Carl Friedrich Gauss (1777–1855) studied the division of the circle, that is the roots of the equation:

$$x^n = 1$$

This led to the theorem that a regular polygon with 17 sides can be constructed with ruler and compasses alone.

48

The parrot flies frantically across and back round her polygon: '119 diagonals,' she squawks.

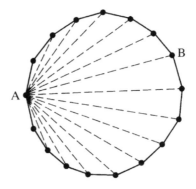

Each point of the edge can be joined to 14 other points across the polygon. So there would be $17 \times 14 = 238$ lines. But you will have counted each line twice (A to B *and* B to A), so in all there are $\frac{238}{2} = 119$ diagonals.

SCORE - **30** - *POINTS*

'You can get a good view of Mathland from the top of that mountain,' promises the parrot. 'Fly up there and see what you can see.'

▶▶ 30

Your weary steps go south once more. After 2 miles you reach the shores of Lake Pythagoras. There is no sign of the ferryman, and you wonder how you will cross the lake.

Nearby an old man sits cross-legged on a dirty old rug. He sees you and his eyes gleam.

'I'll give you my magic carpet,' he says, 'if you can give *me* a Magic Square.'

▶▶ 51

You can have magic cubes too! It is possible to fill in all the numbers from 1 to 27 so that all rows and columns add to 42. So will cube diagonals (but not face diagonals).

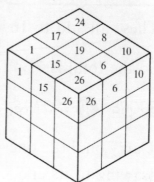

The dragon gets to his feet and examines you more closely.

'Clever little thing, aren't you?' he chuckles.

The number of coins is:

$$1 + 2 + \ldots + 15$$

Split them into pairs:

1 2 3 4 5 6 7   8
15 14 13 12 11 10 9

These all add to 16.   Middle number

So the total is $7 \times 16 + 8 = 120$.

SCORE - **30** - *POINTS*

'Carry on, little one – your journey must be drawing to its end.'

'This is what I want you to do,' continues the man.

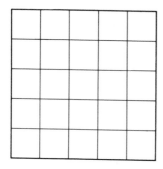

Fill in the numbers from 1 to 25. You may use each number only once. To make the square magic, each row, column or diagonal must add up to the *same* number – the 'magic' number.

When you have found the magic number turn to that page ▶▶

If you need help to complete the square
PAY 10 POINTS ▶▶ 63

52

LOSE 20 POINTS

The largest area is given by a square
6 miles by 6 miles.

Now you should return to the parrot. She
will set you on your path.

 44

If the field does not have to be rectangular, what shape
will give the largest area for a fixed perimeter?

$$3^2 + 4^2 = 5^2$$
$$5^2 + 12^2 = 13^2$$
$$8^2 + 15^2 = 17^2$$

'You had better be on your way,' titters the troll.

What about Pythagorean triplets?

$$1^2 + 6^2 + 8^2 = 2^2 + 4^2 + 9^2$$

Find other sets of three numbers with this property.

LOSE 20 POINTS

You could have found the magic number by a short cut.

$$1 + 2 + \ldots + 25 = ?$$

So how much will each row add up to?

'You have a nice face, so I'll let you borrow my carpet anyway,' mumbles the man.

▶▶ **62**

Magic squares have been around for a long time. The German artist Dürer included this magic square in his engraving 'Melancholia' completed in 1514. It has many amazing properties. Investigate!

16	3	2	13
5	10	11	8
9	6	7	12
4	15	14	1

The knight explains his problem. There is one big square made up of 8 × 8 little squares.

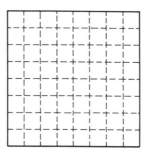

But there are also **?** squares made up of 7 × 7 little squares, and **?** squares made up of 6 × 6 little squares, . . . , and 64 squares made up of 1 × 1 little squares.

How many squares are there in total?

Find the square root of your answer, take the reciprocal, round to 2 significant figures and turn to that page ▶▶

If still stuck on the problem ▶▶ 64

If stuck on the calculation PAY 5 POINTS ▶▶ 74

'There are 28 dominoes in a set,' adjoins the adder, 'so there are 56 numbers on them.'

The numbers 0 to 6 must occur equally often, that is 8 times.

Can you find the number of spots now?

Take the reciprocal of your answer, round to 2 significant figures and turn to that page ▶▶

If still stuck on the problem ▶▶ 46

If stuck on the calculation PAY 5 POINTS ▶▶ 74

You carry on for 3 more miles and once more reach the Fountain of Fermat. This time the gnome does not look at all pleased to see you.

'This is the last puzzle,' he growls.

Using the digits 1 to 6, make two 3-digit numbers which give the largest answer when they are multiplied together.

Multiply the non-zero digits of your answer together, take the square root, round to 2 significant figures and turn to that page ▶▶

If stuck on the problem ▶▶ 67

If stuck on the calculation PAY 5 POINTS ▶▶ 74

'Your map reveals the magic word,'
mouths the Magic Mathematician.

Immediately, in a far corner of the cavern,
the word EXIT appears in red flashing
lights above a door.

SCORE **30** *POINTS*

You step through the door . . .
. . . and out into another adventure.

Find your total score and ▶▶ **73** to see how well you
did.

'Right,' bleats the goat. 'The largest area is a *square* 6 miles by 6 miles.'

SCORE -🔟30- POINTS

'Now you should return to the parrot. She will set you on your path.'

▶▶ 44

Abraham De Moivre (1667–1754) was a pioneer in the fields of algebraic trigonometry and the theory of probability. He was one of the first to use imaginary numbers in trigonometry (imaginary i is the square root of -1), and a formula carries his name:

$$(\cos x + i \sin x)^n = \cos nx + i \sin nx$$

'Well sspotted,' simpers the adder.

There are 28 dominoes in a set, so there will be 56 numbers. The numbers 0 to 6 occur equally often, so they must each appear 8 times.

So the number of spots is:

$$8 (0 + 1 + \ldots + 6)$$
$$= 8 \times 21$$
$$= 168$$

SCORE **30** POINTS

▶▶ 57

The Babylonians used a sexagesimal system for their work on astronomy and mathematics (for example 1, 10, 60, 600, 3600, . . .). Where is this system still used in everyday life?

'Correct,' drools the dragon.
The number of coins is:

$$1 + 2 + \ldots + 12$$

Pair them up:

$$
\begin{array}{cccccc}
1 & 2 & 3 & 4 & 5 & 6 \\
12 & 11 & 10 & 9 & 8 & 7
\end{array}
$$

Each pair adds up to 13.

So the total is $6 \times 13 = 78$.

SCORE ✦ **20** ✦ POINTS

'Carry on with your quest,' directs the
dragon. 'Your journey
must be drawing
to its end.'

▶▶ **49**

62

You leap onto the carpet. It soars into the air and you glide in a south-east direction for nearly 6 miles across Lake Pythagoras.

HINT

Use this triangle to work out how long the other sides will be.

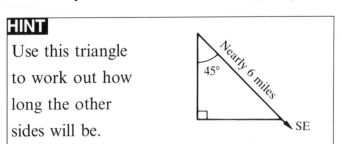

You drop down onto the landing stage,

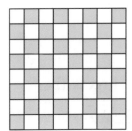

which is patterned like a chessboard. A knight in armour is wandering distractedly to and fro across the board.

'How many? How many?' he keeps asking.

How many different squares, of all sizes, are on the chessboard?

Find the square root of your answer, take the reciprocal, round to 2 significant figures and turn to that page ►►

If stuck on the problem PAY 10 POINTS ►► 55

If stuck on the calculation PAY 5 POINTS ►► 74

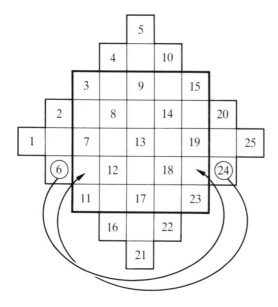

'I have heard,' explains the man, 'that you can start off your square like this. The numbers outside the square each fill in the space *opposite* to them.'

If you have the magic number turn to that page

If you are still stuck ▶▶ 54

64

There should be:

1 square made up of 8 × 8 little squares
4 squares made up of 7 × 7 little squares
9 squares made up of 6 × 6 little squares

. . .

64 squares made up of 1 × 1 little squares

This gives a total of 204 different squares.

The knight throws off his armour and reveals himself as that most awful of monsters – a Maths Teacher!

'Now I can use that puzzle as a Horrible Homework!' he says, as he runs off, chuckling heartily.

 71

Put 12 knights on this chessboard so that every square is occupied or attacked.

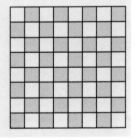

'Magnificent magic number!' cries the man. 'Take my mystical magic carpet.'

65

SCORE  40 POINTS

▶▶ 62

65 is the second number to be a sum of the squares of 2 numbers greater than or equal to zero in 2 different ways:

$$65 = 8^2 + 1^2 = 7^2 + 4^2$$

Find the first and third such numbers.

66

Many travellers have got lost when they left the troll and journeyed to the Mine of Mersenne.

You were travelling north-east and you had to turn *through 45°* (not 135°).

If you can make the password now 72

If your map still does not make sense, then you should return to the start of the maze. You do not need to solve the problems again – use your list of pages visited to help you to redraw the map.

Can you find someone to help you discover what went wrong?

Good hunting! 10

You will make the largest answer if your two numbers are as *large* as possible, and as *equal* as possible. (It's a bit like finding the goat's field.)

'I'm not going to give you the answer,' gurgles the gnome. 'You can try and work it out for yourself.'

You heave a sigh and slip past him. You head south and once more enter the Dark Cavern of Ignorance.

▶▶ 72

68

'But it's easy,' declares the dragon.

The number of coins is:

$$1 + 2 + \ldots + 12$$

Pair them up:

1	2	3	4	5	6
12	11	10	9	8	7

Each pair adds up to 13.
So the total is $6 \times 13 = 78$.

'Carry on with your quest,' directs the dragon. 'Your journey must be drawing to its end.'

▶▶ 49

$$\begin{array}{r} 631 \\ \times\,542 \\ \hline 342\,002 \end{array}$$

SCORE – **30** – POINTS

'Your quest is over,' gurgles the gnome.

You heave a sigh of relief and slip past him.

You head south, and once more enter the Dark Cavern of Ignorance.

▶▶ 72

'At last a solution!' cries the knight.

1 square made up of 8 × 8 little squares

4 squares made up of 7 × 7 little squares

9 squares made up of 6 × 6 little squares

...

64 squares made up of 1 × 1 little squares

This gives a total of 204 different squares.

SCORE *POINTS*

The knight throws off his armour and reveals himself as that most awful of monsters – a Maths Teacher!

'Now I can use that puzzle as a Horrible Homework!' he says, as he runs off, chuckling heartily.

▶▶ 71

You feel somewhat shaken by your ordeal. You trudge south for 1 mile and arrive at the Crossroads of Cantor.

The adder is sitting on a pile of dominoes.

'How many sspots are there on my sset of dominoess?' she hisses.

Take the reciprocal of your answer, round to 2 significant figures and turn to that page ▶▶

If stuck on the problem PAY 10 POINTS ▶▶ 56

If stuck on the calculation PAY 5 POINTS ▶▶ 74

You are back inside the Dark Cavern of Ignorance.

From the depths of the darkness comes the voice of the Magic Mathematician.

'Well, my young friend,' he booms. 'Does your map show you the password for how to escape from here?

'Remember that in Mathland you sometimes have to look at things from a different point of view.'

Score each letter of your password thus:

> A   B   C   D. . . Z
> 1   2   3   4 . . . 26

Find the total score of your word and turn to that page ▶▶

If you are stuck PAY 20 POINTS ▶▶ 66

500 points — Well, you really are a Master Mathematician in your own right. Give the size of your head to the management, and we shall see if the MM's hat can be stretched to fit you. **EXCELLENT**

400 points — You are on your way to becoming a Master Mathematician, even if you are not always perfect. You may borrow the MM's cloak. **PROFICIENT**

300 points — Your progress through the maze has been somewhat higgledy-piggledy, but you got there in the end. You may wear the MM's pointed boots. **CAPABLE**

200 points — You are something of a second-class explorer, being slapdash in your approach. You may darn the MM's socks. **DISMAL**

100 points — You seem to relish being wrong more often than right. You may carry the MM's notebook and pencil – if you promise not to break them. **PATHETIC**

Negative — What can one say? The MM says he will never let you near any of his property. Have you considered being a street-sweeper in Venice? **DISASTROUS**

CALCULATIONS

Each time you use this page you must pay 5 points.

significant figures	Take the first two non-zero digits, starting from the left of your number. Don't forget to round up if the third digit is 5 or more. Just for the purposes of Mathland, ignore any decimal points and minus signs. (Ignore them at your peril elsewhere!)
sin/cos/tan	Make sure that your calculator is working in degrees.
square/square root	Have you used the $\sqrt{}/x^2$ button the correct way round?
reciprocal	This means 1 divided by the number – the $1/x$ button.
cube root	Most scientific calculators have a $^3\sqrt{}$ button. If yours does not, either borrow one or do the following. Does this sequence of operations find $^3\sqrt{8}$ ($= 2$) on your calculator?

$$\boxed{8} \quad \boxed{\text{LOG}} \quad \boxed{\div} \quad \boxed{3} \quad \boxed{=} \quad \boxed{10^x}$$

8 LOG $\div$ 3 $=$ 10^x

If so, try with the number you want.

π	For example, if your answer was 4, then you would take the 3rd and 4th digits of: 3.1 $\boxed{41}$ 592 6 . . . i.e. 41